I LOVE THE LAKE

In East Tennessee

I LOVE THE LAKE

In East Tennessee

Carole Ayres

Crippled Beagle Publishing

This work is protected by the copyright laws of the United States of America. No part of this book may be reproduced or stored, in whole or in part, in print or digital format, without express permission by the author. For information regarding permission, interviews, events, and quotes, write to the publisher.

Crippled Beagle Publishing
5413 Glen Cove Drive, Knoxville, Tennessee 37919
dyer.cbpublishing@gmail.com

©2018 Carole Ayres. All rights reserved.
Photo credits: Carole Ayres
Book design by Jody Dyer

Paddle image: https://pixabay.com/en/paddle-summer-camp-camp-summer-3414020/
Fishing knots: http://flyfishyellowstone.blogspot.com/2009/01/tie-one-on.html

ISBN-13: 978-1-970037-074

Grog's Fishing Knots Index

Albright Knot

Arbor Knot

Blood Knot

Dropper Loop

Improved Clinch

Nail Knot

The Albright Knot is used to join monofilament lines of different sizes. It is often used for example to join the fly line to the fly-reel backing line.

Palomar Knot

Perfection Loop

Rapala Knot

Snell Knot

Double Surgeon's   **Surgeon's Loop**   **Trilene Knot**   **Uni-Knot**

Let's have some fun on the lake!

For my grandchildren.

Every summer we go to the lake.
From the business of home we take a fun break.
Uncles, aunts, and cousins galore,
Don't forget your swimsuits. Let's head to the shore!

Our daily adventures begin at the dock.
We bring goodies and towels and lots of sunblock.
Swim around and feed the fish,
Jump off the pontoon boat,
Whatever you wish.

Every hour of the day we eat and eat.
Because someone's brought down a yummy new treat.
We enjoy chicken, hot dogs, and watermelon.
Friends bring chips and cookies. There's no telling!

It's time to go out on the boat. Take your seats.
While skiing or tubing, we'll see some crazy feats.
Hold onto your drinks and sunglasses.
Grab your hats and hold tight,
As we zoom down the lake clear out of sight!

Load up the tubes. Get ready to go fast.
Everyone scrambles; it's a wild, wet blast!

Circling, flying, and laughing, we hold with all our might.
There go the guys. Their tube's taken flight!

No matter how hard you hold on,
Pretty soon you know you're going to be gone.
Make sure you don't bang your teeth or your head,
On a cousin's knee or elbow; just fall off instead.

Everyone's exhausted,
But no one wants to quit.
So we turn off the boat
To float and just sit.
We compare rope burns,
Cuts and bruises,
As the captain takes a break
And just cruises.

Back to the dock we go to load the boat with more treats.
Hurry up everyone. Quickly, take your seats!
We head out again to say goodbye to the day,
Tired but thankful, we watch the last rays.

Today we traveled the lake miles and miles.
In the shimmering light we see sun-kissed smiles.
Slowly we head home in the dark.
Gently, Captain Joe cuts the motor and pulls in to park.

I'm really tired.
I can't eat another bite.
I'm going to bed, y'all.
God bless and goodnight.

See you in the morning.
I hope a good night's rest
You 'll spend,
When we wake up tomorrow,
We'll do it all again!

About the Author

Carole Ayres lives in Tennessee with her husband Joe. She is a retired teacher who travels the world. When she is home, Carole tutors young people and spends time serving her church and playing outdoors with her grandchildren.

Look for other *I LOVE* books by Carole Ayres on Amazon.com, Kindle, and at a variety of retailers. For information on future titles, book signings, quotes, excerpts, and interviews, write to:

Crippled Beagle Publishing, 5413 Glen Cove Drive
Knoxville, Tennessee 37919
dyer.cbpublishing@gmail.com

www.ingramcontent.com/pod-product-compliance
Lightning Source LLC
Chambersburg PA
CBHW040011080526
44586CB00028B/2966